*These
Numbered
Days*

Peter Huchel

These Numbered Days

Gezählte Tage
(1972)

*translated from German
by Martyn Crucefix*

Shearsman Books

First published in the United Kingdom in 2019 by
Shearsman Books
50 Westons Hill Drive
Emersons Green
BRISTOL
BS16 7DF

Shearsman Books Ltd Registered Office
30–31 St. James Place, Mangotsfield, Bristol BS16 9JB
(this address not for correspondence)

www.shearsman.com

ISBN 978-1-84861-660-8

TRANSLATOR'S NOTE
*I would like to thank Marion Adler for her invaluable help in the early stages
of this translation. Thanks also to Hub Nijssen, Radboud University,
Netherlands, and Iain Galbraith for advice and assistance in the latter stages.
Of course, any errors that remain are all my own.*

The translation of this work was supported
by a grant given by the Goethe-Institut, London.

Contents

III

IV

v

Introduction

Peter Huchel (1903-1981) is a one-off in the poetry landscape of modern Germany. A poet that deserves to be mentioned in the tradition of the greats of twentieth-century German poetry: Rilke, Trakl, Brecht, Gottfried Benn, Paul Celan and sharing something with all of them. Indeed, Joseph Brodsky set him alongside Benn as one of the greatest German poets of the modern age. But he is a poet who remains curiously unknown outside Germany. Perhaps that has something to do with his biography: he lived through two world wars and fell victim to the division of Germany after 1945. As a consequence, his writing life was pitched against the twin threats of silence and political dogma, notably during the years he spent in the former GDR, or East Germany. Gripped in that terrible vice, he published only four collections of poetry. But there are also more quintessential reasons for his relative obscurity: the fact that his poetry invites associations with various opposing groupings – the sceptical poets of the 1950s in the East (Johannes Bobrowski, Erich Arendt, Günter Kunert), or the accomplished 'unpolitical' nature poets in the tradition of Oskar Loerke, Wilhelm Lehmann, and Elisabeth Langgässer. Yet he sits uneasily in either of these or indeed other familiar categories. He is a nature poet but never one for rural idyll, an elegist with a critical eye, a mythmaker with a commitment to the particularity of things, a political poet but one who never abandons the lyric impulse. Finally, he is a poet for whom every word seems to be wrested from and threatened by silence.

He was born, Hellmut Huchel, into a middle-class family in a suburb of Berlin, Lichterfelde, in 1903, but spent his formative childhood years on his grandfather's farm at Alt-Langewisch in rural Brandenburg, an experience which would mark his works for the rest of his life and to which he would return as a core of his poetry. In the tinderbox atmosphere after the First World War, aged seventeen he became briefly involved with the conservative Kapp-Putsch against the Weimar Republic in 1920, but wounded during the violence and hospitalised, he came to develop the left-wing sympathies that would mark his life. He studied at the universities of Berlin, Freiburg and Vienna, and spent time travelling to France, Italy, Greece, Hungary, Romania, Turkey. In 1930, he changed his first name to Peter. His early poems date back to his student days and bear witness to his younger years in Brandenburg. On the surface they seem conventional nature lyrics, using traditional metre and rhyme. On closer inspection though, this is a natural world marked by poverty, hard work and brutality, with a distinctive sympathy for the lot of Brandenburg's peasants. It was in his student days that his first poems appeared in print and he was awarded the prize of the left-leaning *Kolonne* journal for poetry in 1932. But here history was to intervene once again with the rise of Hitler. Uncomfortable that his poetry might be associated with the atavistic Nationalist Socialist 'blood and soil' aesthetic, he turned inwards (as he would in later life, under political pressure in the GDR). He returned to Brandenburg and isolated himself in a kind of inner emigration until he was drafted in 1941 and served in the Luftwaffe on the eastern front, ending up a Russian prisoner of war.

With the fall of the Third Reich, Huchel saw the Soviet zone of influence as a chance for a new German beginning, cleansed of the atrocities of Nazi Germany and promising a truly humane future. He returned, like many of his compatriots (Bertolt Brecht from the USA and Johannes R. Becher from Russia) to build that new society. In Huchel's case this involved a job as dramaturge and later artistic director of Berlin Radio, a post he held until 1948. That same year he published his first volume of poems *Gedichte (Poems)*. Huchel always had an uncomfortable relationship with the authorities both in his work and his own writing. With his dark rural poems steeped in 'Naturmagie' (nature magic), their exclamatory energy and almost Expressionist imagery sat oblique to the cool functional socialist realist norms and did little to endorse the future-oriented technological vision of the young socialist society.

Nevertheless, in 1949 he became editor-in-chief of the leading cultural journal *Sinn und Form (Sense and Form)*. This East German periodical was founded by the first Cultural Minister of the GDR Johannes R. Becher, and became a landmark publication in East Germany. This was largely down to the period of Huchel's brave and single-minded editorship, which saw an outward-looking internationalism and publication of writers that challenged the status quo, to such an extent that the journal, despite its official status, could be simultaneously described by Walter Jens as 'the secret journal of the nation'.

But this set Huchel on an inevitable course of conflict with the state, only exacerbated by his joining calls for freedom in publishing. He managed to walk a tightrope for thirteen years in total, partly on account of Brecht's support, but after the building of the Berlin Wall, there was no room for a demonstrably liberal journal of this kind and in 1962 Huchel was forcibly removed from his position and publicly censured. The final edition of the journal under his editorship was a calculated riposte to the authorities, entirely characteristic of Huchel's tactical resistance: publishing Brecht's 'On Reason's Powers of Resistance', contributions by Paul Celan and Günter Eich, Sartre, Aragon, Yevtushenko, Hans Mayer, Ernst Fischer and others (all calculated to provoke the authorities) and ending with six of his own poems (including 'The Garden of Theophrastus' and 'Winter-psalm').

The poem 'The Garden of Theophrastus' (not included in this collection) might be thought of almost as an epitaph for Huchel; but is instructive also for what his poetry can do at its best. It remembers Theophrastus, the Greek philosopher scientist and humanist with his botanical interests; and in this we can read too Huchel's own husbandry of poetry in the GDR. But now the garden is dead, the lyric subject's breathing is heavier; all is threatened by an anonymous, external power (in Michael Hamburger's translation):

> An olive tree splits the brickwork grown brittle
> And still is a voice in the mote-laden heat.
> Their order was to fell and uproot it,
> Your light is fading, defenceless leaves.

Here nature has become a symbol of political events; the poem was written in 1961 and published in the West in 1963. At first it seems like the external forces have triumphed: the fading light, the defenceless leaves. And yet anyone reading in 1961 will scarcely have been able to ignore the explosive power of the word 'Mauer' (wall) contained within 'Gemäuer', translated here by Michael Hamburger as brickwork. What is more: the tree splits the stone, and still echoes as a voice in the scorching heat. But, more than that, the poem invites posterity to remember 'the vanished who planted their conversations like trees' and in that concretely recalls Brecht in exile from Fascism (his famous poem to posterity, 'To those born after') and the voices of poetry threatened by silence. In short, the poem finely balances natural world, reflection, allegory and memories of the past, but also enacts its own promise: a tribute to the fragile but lasting possibilities of poetic resistance that resonate within it.

With his own departure from the scene, Huchel withdrew to almost complete isolation, pretty much under house arrest in Wilhelmshorst, near Potsdam, and began nine years of inner emigration once again. This was a life under constant observation by the Stasi, or secret police, and filled with petty reprisals that took a toll on his health. His telephones were bugged, his post intercepted, his archive forcibly removed, and opportunities to publish thwarted. This is captured in the poem 'Hubertusweg':

> He stands down there,
> wretched as stale tobacco smoke,
> my neighbour, my shadow
> on my heels as I leave the house.

Notwithstanding these pressures the house became a centre for like-minded, alienated writers from East and West, continuing the conversations across the political divide. One of those, Wolf Biermann, dedicated his famous song 'Ermutigung' ('Encouragement') to Huchel: 'My friend, don't let yourself be hardened / in these hard times of ours'. Huchel's next collection *Chausseen Chausseen* (*Highways Highways*, 1963), however, could appear only in West Germany and that in defiance of the GDR authorities. It is a catalogue of a bleak and dismal existence in terse free verse forms, constantly on the edge of silence. After a long campaign he was finally permitted to leave the GDR and, after a spell in Italy, at the Villa Massimo, he settled near Freiburg, on the edge of the Black Forest. The honours that West Germany paid him in the 1960s continued, including the Europalia-Prize, inaugurated in 1977 and of which he was the first recipient. At first he gave regular public readings, but encroaching illness gradually immobilised him. This went hand in hand with a spiritual darkening and he found himself alienated by the brutality and materialism of unapologetic capitalism. He published two further collections: *Gezählte Tage* (*These Numbered Days*) in 1972 which gathered the poems written in isolation in Wilhelmshorst and *Die neunte Stunde* (*The Ninth Hour*) in 1979. This last book, as Martyn Crucefix says, 'is a book almost exclusively of elegy and lament; the ninth hour is the hour of despair, the hour in which Christ is said to have died on the Cross, crying out, "My God, my God, why have you forsaken me?"' Huchel himself died in 1981, aged 78, having found himself alienated, exiled and silenced in three German states.

Notwithstanding this, his voice, indeed his legacy lives on in the Peter Huchel Prize for German-language poetry, founded in 1984; the Peter Huchel house, now a writers' centre; in the work of younger poets such as Lutz Seiler, himself also onetime director and custodian at the Peter Huchel Museum in Wilhelmshorst, and in some forty radio plays, essays and four slim but resonant books of poetry.

In presenting *These Numbered Days* for publication Martyn Crucefix has picked a body of work which gives us a taste of Huchel at his richest, but also speaks powerfully to our time. There is the almost universal sense of winter in the volume: the fog, snow and ice and the threadbare existences that struggle through them. There is the familiar sense of threat: 'A hoof still / beats the hour. / And by morning / the sky-wide shriek of crows'. ('Arrival'). Everywhere the threat of counted days, time running out. In 'Before Nîmes 1452', a poem about the exiled François Villon, these things come together:

> Are these the years
> assigned to you?
>
> Are these the crows
> that are coming slowly closer
> to tear you to pieces?

The hint here of a mythological projection of self (Prometheus tied to the rock and punished by authority) also demonstrates Huchel widening his range to include poems on mythical and legendary figures: Ulysses and Undine appear as well as Ophelia and Macbeth. As the very helpful notes to this volume also make clear, the poems are often refracted through Biblical quotations too. And if one can never truly be sure about Huchel's religious position, there is certainly a kind of spiritual dimension in the attention he gives the world around him.

The backdrop is always of the natural world, but often pressed hard into allegory. His use of a favourite core vocabulary contributes at once to the overriding intensity of the volume but also the sense of no escape. As is perhaps to be expected, the volume constantly comes back to his own isolation and precarious survival: 'the knack' of persisting in a hostile environment:

> The knack
> of poet-spiders—
> to spin from their own
> substance a thin wire

on which to balance
adroitly with two faces,
a single feather,
whatever the breeze.

The phrase from the title poem, *these numbered days*, might well refer to
the nine long years spent in Wilhelmshorst; they might indicate a sober
reckoning with aging, illness and mortality; or how long one might survive
a game of two faces, but they also speak to a larger sense of time running
out in our day to day existence as witnessed also in Ingeborg Bachmann's
resonant *Mortgaged Time* (*Die gestundete Zeit*), published in 1953.

But the collection is not entirely without hope. There is always an
attempt to reach back to a better way of being (perhaps that untouched
memory of childhood) or to reach down to the roots that connect the
natural world with a darker realm, of earth, death, and memory. And
to fetch something back from there that will counter the misery of the
moment. A poem 'The Dipper' gives some sense of what might come
out of that attention and that reaching down. Watching the bird swoop
down through alder, to the stony river bed to fetch its food, the lyric
subject reflects on his own lot:

If I could plunge
brighter downwards
into the flowing darkness

about me to fish out a word

like this dipper
beside the alder boughs
picks its food

from the stony river bed.

Gold-panner, fisherman,
relinquish all your gear.
The shy bird

looks to work without a sound.

The poem then bids the fisherman and gold-panners on the riverbank to still their noisy, clumsy clamour. This is work to be done in silence. Striking here is the subjunctive mood which seems to launch into the foreign element, just like the dipper itself, in a mode which is as much natural as almost prayer. The poem demonstrates much about Huchel's poetic universe: the simple vocabulary; the specificity (dipper, alder); the attention (that suggestive 'brighter'); the sparseness in which the whiteness around the words plays a full part in the poem. The exquisite sound echoes in Martyn Crucefix's translation (dipper, flowing, pick, fish, relinquish) seem to ripple through the poem like the dipper through water. Then there is the sleek reaching down through darkness, undergrowth, roots, water, stones, to the core of things to fetch up something perfect, 'a word'.

That we know of Huchel's poetry at all is largely thanks to the invaluable early work by Michael Hamburger who first translated him in 1974 and continued to champion his work until the appearance of *The Garden of Theophrastus and other Poems* with Anvil Press in 2004. Nevertheless, it is high time to see another angle on his poetry in English and Martyn Crucefix provides just the lightness of touch but also the austerity needed. Indeed, knowing Martyn's work as I do it is not so very hard to see a spiritual affinity here, which has resulted in pitch-perfect translation as intense and yet particular as the originals. We have another reason to be grateful to Martyn Crucefix and Shearsman Books. Read today beyond the political climate of the Cold War, we see Huchel with fresh urgency. The poet we encounter is severe and elegiac, sensual and attentive, constantly fetching up those perfect, the Germans would say lapidary, verses out of the darkness. But those bright words held up to view as talismans against unaccountable and corrupt powers, ecological threat, approaching darkness, the sense of impending disaster, these truly feel like poems for these, our own, numbered days.

Karen Leeder
Oxford, 2019

Select Bibliography

Gedichte (1948)
Chausseen, Chausseen. Gedichte (1963)
Die Sternenreuse. Gedichte 1925-1947 (1968)
Gezählte Tage. Gedichte (1972)
Die neunte Stunde. Gedichte (1979)
Die Gedichte (1997)
Gesammelte Werke in 2 Bänden (2017)

Best, Otto F., ed., *Hommage für Peter Huchel*, Zum 3. April 1968, Munich: Piper, 1968.

Freytag, Cornelia, *Weltsituationen in der Lyrik Peter Huchels*, Frankfurt: Lang, 1998.

Mayer, Hans, ed., *Über Peter Huchel*, Frankfurt: Shrkamp, 1973.

Nijssen, Hub, *Der heimliche König: Leben und Werk von Peter Huchel*, Nijmegen University Press, 1995; Königshausen & Neumann Verlag, Würzburg 1998.

Nijssen, Hub, ed., *Wie will man da Gedichte schreiben*. Briefe 1925-1977, Frankfurt am Main, 2000.

Schoor, Uwe, *Das Geheime Journal der Nation. Die Zeitschrift* Sinn und Form, Chefredakteur; Peter Huchel 1949-1962. Berlin, Bern, Frankfurt a.M., 1992.

Siemes, Christof, *Das Testament gestürzter Tannen. Das lyrische Werk Peter Huchels*, Freiburg im Breisgau: Rombach, 1996.

Vieregg, Axel, ed., *Peter Huchel*, Suhrkamp Taschenbuch Materialien, Frankfurt: Suhrkamp, 1986.

Walther, Peter, ed., *Peter Huchel: Leben und Werk*, Frankfurt: Insel, 1996.

English Translations

The Garden of Theophrastus and other poems, translated by Michael Hamburger, Anvil Press, 2004.

The Wilson Quarterly, Winter, 1994, pp. 100-107, includes fourteen poems by Huchel, selected and introduced by Joseph Brodsky, translated by Joel Spector.

On Crutches of Naked Poplars, translated by Robert Firmage. *Mid-American Review* Vol. XI, no. 1, 1991, p. 137-187.

A Thistle In His Mouth: Poems by Peter Huchel, selected, translated and introduced by Henry Beissel, Cormorant Books, Dunvegan, Ontario 1987.

Peter Huchel: Selected Poems, translated by Michael Hamburger. Cheadle, 1974.

Secondary Works in English

Dolan, Joseph P., "The Politics of Peter Huchel's Early Verse," *University of Dayton Review* 13, no. 2 (1978).

Flores, John, *Poetry in East Germany: Adjustments, Visions, and Provocations, 1945-1970,* Yale University Press, 1971.

Hamburger, Michael, *The Truth of Poetry,* 1969; Penguin Books, 1972.

Hilton, Ian, "Peter Huchel's Poetic Vision," in *Neue Ansichten: The Reception of Romanticism in the Literature of the GDR,* eds. Gaskill, Howard, et al., Amsterdam and Atlanta, Georgia: Rodopi, 1990.

Hilton, Ian: Peter Huchel. *Plough a lonely furrow.* Lochee Publications, Blairgowrie, 1986.

Parker, Stephen, "Collected—Recollected—Uncollected? Peter Huchel's *Gesammelte Werke,*" in *German Life and Letters* 40, no. 1 (1986).

Parker, Stephen, "Visions, Revisions and Divisions: The Critical Legacy of Peter Huchel," in *German Life and Letters* 41, no. 2 (1988).

Parker, Stephen, "Peter Huchel and 'Sinn und Form': The German Academy of Arts and the Issue of German Cultural Unity," in *German Writers and the Cold War, 1945-61,* edited by Williams, Rhys W., et al., Manchester and New York: Manchester University Press, 1992.

Parker, Stephen, *Peter Huchel: A Literary Life in 20th-Century Germany,* Bern: Lang, 1998.

Vieregg, Axel, "The Truth about Peter Huchel?" in *German Life and Letters* 41, no. 2 (1988).

Yuille, Nicolas, *Visionary Poetry in the German Dictatorships: Peter Huchel and Johannes Bobrowski,* University of Manchester, 2014.

I

I

Ophelia

Später, am Morgen,
gegen die weiße Dämmerung hin,
das Waten von Stiefeln
im seichten Gewässer,
das Stoßen von Stangen,
ein rauhes Kommando,
sie heben die schlammige
Stacheldrahtreuse.

Kein Königreich,
Ophelia,
wo ein Schrei
das Wasser höhlt,
ein Zauber
die Kugel
am Weidenblatt zersplittern läßt.

Antwort

Zwischen zwei Nächten
der kurze Tag.
Es bleibt das Gehöft.
Und eine Falle, die uns
im Dickicht der Jäger stellt.

Die Mittagsöde.
Noch wärmt sie den Stein.
Gezirp im Wind,
das Schwirren einer Gitarre
den Hang hinab.

Die Lunte
aus welkem Laub
glimmt an der Mauer.

Ophelia

Later, come morning,
against the white of sunrise,
wading boots
through shallow waters,
the probing of sticks,
a curt command,
they lift out a muddied
snare of barbed wire.

No kingdom,
Ophelia,
where one cry
hollows the water,
one spell
and the bullet
splinters on a willow leaf.

Answer

Between two nights
comes brief day.
The farmyard remains.
And for us, a trap set
in the brake by the hunter.

Midday's desolation.
It still warms the stone.
A chirp in the wind,
the burring of a guitar
down the hillside.

Fuse-wires
of withered leaves
glint on the wall.

Salzweiße Luft.
Pfeilspitzen des Herbstes,
Kranichzüge.

Im hellen Geäst
verhallt der Stundenschlag.
Spinnen legen
aufs Räderwerk
die Schleier toter Bräute.

Unterm Sternbild des Hercules

Eine Ortschaft,
nicht größer
als der Kreis,
den abends am Himmel
der Bussard zieht.

Eine Mauer,
rauh behauen, brandig
von rötlichem Moos.
Ein Glockenton,
der über schimmernde Wasser
den Rauch
der Oliven trägt.
Feuer,
von Halmen genährt
und nassem Laub,
durchweht von Stimmen,
die du nicht kennst.

Schon in die Nacht gebeugt,
ins eisige Geschirr,
schleppt Hercules
die Kettenegge der Sterne
den nördlichen Himmel hinauf.

Salt-white air.
Arrowheads of autumn,
the flight of cranes.

In bright boughs
the hour's pulse subsides.
Spiders deploy
their rims and spokes,
the veils of dead brides.

Under the Constellation of Hercules

A settlement,
no larger
than the circle
a buzzard traces
in the evening sky.

A stone wall,
rough-cut, scorched
with rusted moss.
A bell note,
across the glittering water
smoke carries
from the olives.
Fire,
fed by stems
and wet leaves,
cut through with voices,
none of which you know.

Bent already by the night
into his icy harness,
Hercules drags
the stars' chain-harrow
up the northern sky.

Ankunft

Männer mit weißen
zerfetzten Schärpen
reiten am Rand des Himmels
den Scheunen zu,
Einkehr suchend
für eine Nacht,
wo die Sibyllen
wohnen im Staub der Sensen.

Grünfüßig
hängt das Teichhuhn
am Pfahl.
Wer wird es rupfen?
Wer zündet im blakenden Nebel
das Feuer an?
Weh der verlorenen
Krone von Ephraim,
der welken Blume
am Messerbalken der Mähmaschine,
der Nacht
auf kalter Tenne.

Ein Huf
schlägt noch die Stunde an.
Und gegen Morgen
am Himmel ein Krähengeschrei.

Arrival

Men in white
ripped sashes
ride the rim of the sky
towards the barns
in search of lodging,
one night only,
where the Sibyls
live in the scythes' dust.

Green-footed
the moorhen hangs
from a stake.
Who'll pluck it?
Who kindles a bonfire
under the smoking fog?
Woe to the lost
crown of Ephraim,
to the withered flower
in the blades of the mower,
to night
on the cold threshing floor.

A hoof still
beats the hour.
And by morning
the sky-wide shriek of crows.

Exil

Am Abend nahen die Freunde,
die Schatten der Hügel.
Sie treten langsam über die Schwelle,
verdunkeln das Salz,
verdunkeln das Brot
und führen Gespräche mit meinem Schweigen.

Draußen im Ahorn
regt sich der Wind:
Meine Schwester, das Regenwasser
in kalkiger Mulde,
gefangen
blickt sie den Wolken nach.

Geh mit dem Wind,
sagen die Schatten.
Der Sommer legt dir
die eiserne Sichel aufs Herz.
Geh fort, bevor im Ahornblatt
das Stigma des Herbstes brennt.

Sei getreu, sagt der Stein.
Die dämmernde Frühe
hebt an, wo Licht und Laub
ineinander wohnen
und das Gesicht
in einer Flamme vergeht.

Exile

Come evening, friends close in,
the shadows of hills.
Slowly they press across the threshold,
darkening the salt,
darkening the bread
and with my silence they strike up a conversation.

Outside in the maple
the wind stirs:
my sister, the rainwater
in the chalky trough,
imprisoned,
gazes up at the clouds.

Fly with the wind,
say the shadows.
The summer lays
its iron sickle on your heart.
Go now, before the maple leaf burns
with the brand of autumn.

Stay faithful, says the stone.
The dawning sun
ascends, where light and leafage
twine one with another
and vision
goes up in flames.

Die Gaukler Sind Fort

Sie gingen
lautlos dem weißen Wasser nach.
Der Fähnrich und das Mädchen,
der bucklige Händler mit Ketten und Ringen,
sie alle sind fort.
Es blieb der Hügel,
wo sie sich trafen,
die Eiche, mächtig gegabelt,
in grüner Wipfelwildnis.

Mittags,
unter der Wärme des Steins,
hörst du Orgelklänge,
und eine Maske, maulbeerfarben,
weht durchs Gebüsch.

Die Eiche, mächtig gegabelt,
die den Donner barg –
in morscher Kammer des Baums
schlafen die Fledermäuse,
drachenhäutig.
Die hochberühmten Gaukler sind fort.

Die Viper

Schöne Viper,
die Elster flog durch deinen Schlaf
und stahl dir das Gold aus den Augenwinkeln.

Starren Hauptes,
auf schartigem Schädel,
wo Olegs Pferd
in Fäulnis brennt,
erwartest du die Nacht.

The Players Have Gone

Without a word
they followed the white water.
The flag-bearer and young girl,
the hump-backed trader with rings and chains,
they're all gone now.
The hillside remains,
where they assembled,
the oak tree, massively split
in the green wilderness of its crown.

At midday,
among the warmth of the stones,
you catch sounds of an organ,
and a mask, mulberry-coloured,
slips through the bushes.

The oak, massively split,
that took upon itself the thunder—
in the rotten core of the tree
the bats slumber,
dragon-scaled.
The world-famous players have gone.

The Viper

Beautiful viper,
the magpie flew through your sleep
and stole gold from the corner of your eye.

Goggling head,
on a jagged skull,
where Oleg's nag
smoulders while it rots,
you wait for nightfall.

Sie kommt aus dichtem Birkengehölz,
bernsteinäugig,
die Freundin der Fledermäuse.
Sie füllt mit bitterer Milch
die Löwenzahnröhre.

An der Lachswasserbucht
Für Jean Améry

Dies ist dein Rastplatz,
alter Mann,
ein Ahorngerippe.

Noch wärmt die Sonne
deine Hand, noch spürst du
den Flossenschlag des Himmels
im wäßrigen Nebel
der Lachswasserbucht.

Die Stille trat
in den Schatten der Felsen
und blieb verborgen.
Kein Ruderstoß, kein Knirschen der Boote
im mehligen Licht der Dämmerung.

Und keiner kommt,
die Rute geschultert,
und watet
im grauen Kiesbett des Stroms
die Schlucht hinauf.
Es blickt dich
der Wald mit den Augen
des Marders an.

It advances from a thick stand of birches,
amber-eyed,
the lover of bats.
It loads the stalks of dandelions
with bitter milk.

Beside the Salmon Pool

for Jean Améry

This is your resting place,
old man,
a skin-and-bone maple.

Yet the sun warms
your hand, still you sense
the fin's pulse of air
in the wet mist
of the salmon pool.

Silence stepped
into the shade of the rocks
and remained hidden.
No oar's thump, no rasp of boats
in dawn's chalk-light.

And no-one comes
with a shouldered rod,
nobody wades
the stream's grey gravel bed
along the valley.
Gazing at you,
the forest with the eyes
of martens.

Pensione Cigolini

Im Fensterviereck
das stäubende Meer,
in sinkender Sonne
die Farben mischend,
die uns erinnern
an ein Gespräch
im Wechsel
von Wind und Wolken,
bis uns das Salz
die Lippen verschloß.

Im Fensterviereck
die spät geschnittene
Rose im Glas
wie eine Wunde in der Luft.
Wer stieß den Speer?
Mit leeren Booten
fährt der Abend aus.

Venedig im Regen

Noch im Nebel
leuchtet das Gold des Löwen,
das steinerne Laubwerk tropft.
Namen, meergeboren,
wer schrieb sie ins salzige Licht?
Keiner nennt
die große Geduld
der Pfähle.

Auf die Fähre
wartend im Regen,
der Poren
ins Wasser schlägt,

Pensione Cigolini

In a square window
the flecked ocean,
in the descending sun
a blur of colours
that reminds us
of conversations
through the exchange
of wind and cloud,
until salt
locked tight our lips.

In a square window
the lately picked
rose in a glass
like a wound in the air.
Who hurled the spear?
Evening passing away
on the empty barges.

Venice in Rain

Even in fog
the gold of the lion gleams,
the stone leaf-work dribbling.
Names, sea-born,
who inscribed them in the salty light?
No-one talks
of the long patience
of the piles.

Loitering in the rain
for the ferry-boat,
pores hammered open
in the water,

blick ich hinüber
zu den rostigen Schiffen
der Giudecca.

Die Seekarten schweigen.
Es schweigt
die Muschel
am Nacken des Steins.

Mittag in Succhivo
Für Gottfried Bermann Fischer

Es ist Mittag.
Und wieder die Stimme
hinter dem Felsen:
Nicht stoße der Fuß
an den dünnen Schatten
der Distel.

Es ist Mittag
die Gärten hinab –
er heftet helle Fäden
ins staubige Grau der Oliven.
Er wird die Drossel
nicht fangen.

Es ist Mittag.
Er stellt den gelben Krug an die Mauer
und speichert die Hitze
auf flachen Dächern,
als schnitten die Antennen
durch Wasserglanz.

Die Küstenstraße. Härter
hebt sich das Licht in die Stunde.
Das felsige Riff,
das Haupt der Öde.
Es ist Mittag.
Die Meeresstille der Gedanken.

I gaze across
towards the rusting vessels
of Giudecca.

The sea maps say nothing.
Nothing to say
the mussels
slung round the neck of the stone

Midday in Succhivo
for Gottfried Bermann Fischer

It's midday.
And that voice again
from beyond the rocks:
don't thrust a foot
into the paltry shade
of the thistle.

It's midday
all down the gardens—
securing bright threads
to the dusty grey of olives.
He'll not trap
the thrush.

It's midday.
He sets a yellow jug by the wall
and stokes the heat
on flat roofs
as if aerials scythe
through the glitter of water.

The coast road. Hardening
light gathers by the hour.
The rocky reef,
the main of desolation.
It's midday.
The flat calm of reflection.

Subiaco

Stadt,
verschwistert
der heiteren Klarheit der Berge,
am Rand der Felsen der Klosterhimmel.
Unter den schrundigen Stämmen
der Maulbeerbäume im Hof
der harte Glanz einer Schaufel,
er will die Toten ausgraben.

An der weißen Mauer
schreitet der Mönch die Treppe hinauf,
Schweiß sickert durch seine Augenbrauen.

Alles verblaßt in Licht und Hitze,
der grobe Ocker der Wände,
das spröde zerbrechliche Moos auf den Steinen,
das spärliche Grün am Fluß.
Der Glöckner geht in zerrissenen Leinenschuhen,
bald wird der Mittag hallen.

Die Ziege stößt
mit den Hörnern die Sonne fort
und sucht den dünnen Schatten.
Die Schüssel des Pilatus ist ohne Wasser,
er kann seine Hände nicht waschen.

Subiaco

Town,
twinned
with the bright clarity of the mountains,
its sky-high monastery on a cliff-edge.
Under the pockmarked trunks
of mulberry trees in the yard
the hard glint of a shovel,
one looking to unearth the dead.

Beside the whitewashed wall
a monk clambers up steps,
sweat trickling from his brows.

Everything fades in light and heat,
the rough ochre of walls,
the fragile, scant moss on stones,
the sparse green by the river.
The bell-ringer walks in ripped canvas shoes,
soon midday will sound.

The goat fends off
sunlight with its horns
and roots through thin shade.
Pilate's bowl stands emptied of water,
impossible to wash his hands.

II

II

Gezählte Tage

Gezählte Tage, Stimmen, Stimmen,
vorausgesandt durch Sonne und Wind
und im Gefolge rasselnder Blätter,
noch ehe der Fluß
den Nebel speichert im Schilf.

Vergiß die Stadt,
wo unter den Hibiskusbäumen
das Maultier morgens gesattelt wird,
der Gurt gezogen, die Tasche gepackt,
die Frauen stehn am Küchenfeuer,
wenn noch die Brunnen im Regen schlafen.
Vergiß den Weg,
betäubt vom Duft des Pfeifenstrauchs,
die schmale Tür,
wo unter der Matte der Schlüssel liegt.

Zwei Schatten,
Rücken an Rücken,
zwei Männer warten im frostigen Gras.
Stunde,
die nicht mehr deine Stunde ist,
Stimmen,
vorausgesandt durch Nebel und Wind.

These Numbered Days

These numbered days—voices, voices,
sent on ahead through sun and wind
and the rattling wake of leaves,
before the river
stows fog among the reeds.

So forget the town,
where under hibiscus trees
the mule is saddled in the morning,
its girth tightened, saddlebags full,
women gathering round the kitchen stove,
where wells slumber still in rain.
Forget the path,
stunned by the odour of philadelphus,
the narrow doorway,
where the key lies under a mat.

Two shadows,
back to back—
two men loitering on the frosty grass.
Hour,
that is no longer your hour,
voices,
sent on ahead through fog and wind.

Nachlässe

Nachlässe,
ungeordnet,
auf Böden verstaubt,
die Erben sind tot.
Und finstere Himmel,
grau unterkellert
von Wänden aus Nebel.
Die Kälte atmet
in hallenden Gängen.

Später,
im Sommer
über den Stoppeln
die Spindeln aus Licht.
Sie wickeln
das rissige Garn
galizischer Dörfer.
Doch niemand kommt,
den Mantel zu weben.

Durchbrüche,
verschüttet,
von Keller zu Keller,
das letzte Verlies
zwei Kannen in Warschau,
vergraben
in Erde und Feuer.
Es geht durch Wolken
stürzender Asche
die Stimme hinab,
die Erben zu rufen.

Estates

Estates,
disordered,
dust across the floor,
the heirs dead.
And grim skies,
grey basements,
fog for walls.
Cold breathes
in the echoing passageways.

Later,
in summertime
across the stubble,
spindles of light.
They gather up
the fraying threads
of Galician villages.
But none comes
to weave a coat.

Breached,
each barricaded,
cellar after cellar,
the last dungeon,
two churns in Warsaw
interred
in earth and fire.
Out of the clouds
of tumbling ash,
a voice descends
summoning the heirs.

Hahnenkämme

Eines Abends, nach dem Markt,
bot mir eine Alte
zwei junge Hähne an.
Gebündelt,
die Füße gefesselt,
den Kopf nach unten,
hingen sie
schlaff
an erdiger Hand.
Ich ging vorüber.

Hinter den Pfählen
an der Bucht
sah ich im Widerschein der sinkenden Sonne
die Hahnenkämme gezackter Felsen
im Wasser leuchten.

Die Wasseramsel

Könnte ich stürzen
heller hinab
ins fließende Dunkel

um mir ein Wort zu fischen,

wie diese Wasseramsel
durch Erlenzweige,
die ihre Nahrung

vom steinigen Grund des Flusses holt.

Goldwäscher, Fischer,
stellt eure Geräte fort.
Der scheue Vogel

will seine Arbeit lautlos verrichten.

Cockscombs

One evening, after market,
an old woman offered
two young roosters.
All trussed up,
their feet tied,
heads to the ground,
they hung
limp
in her earthy hand.
I walked on.

Beyond the piers
of the bay
I catch in the reflection of the sinking sun,
cockscombs of jagged rocks
lit up in the water.

The Dipper

If I could plunge
brighter downwards
into the flowing darkness

about me to fish out a word

like this dipper
beside the alder boughs
picks its food

from the stony river bed.

Gold-panner, fisherman,
relinquish all your gear.
The shy bird

looks to work without a sound.

Ölbaum und Weide

Im schroffen Anstieg brüchiger Terrassen
dort oben der Ölbaum,
am Mauerrand
der Geist der Steine,
noch immer
die leichte Brandung
von grauem Silber in der Luft,
wenn Wind die blasse Unterseite
des Laubs nach oben kehrt.

Der Abend wirft sein Fangnetz ins Gezweig.
Die Urne aus Licht
versinkt im Meer.
Es ankern Schatten in der Bucht.

Sie kommen wieder, verschwimmend im Nebel,
durchtränkt
vom Schilfdunst märkischer Wiesen,
die wendischen Weidenmütter,
die warzigen Alten
mit klaffender Brust,
am Rand der Teiche,
der dunkeläugig verschlossenen Wasser,
die Füße in die Erde grabend,
die mein Gedächtnis ist.

Die Töpferinsel

Hinter uns der eisige Vogel
mit weißen Schwingen,
den Schneewind,
das nasse Segel
aufs Wasser drückend.

Olive Tree and Willow

On the steeply raked crumbling terraces
there, the olive,
the spirit of stone
beside a wall,
yet always
the light surge
of silvery-grey in the air
where the pallid undersides
of leaves are turned by the breeze.

Evening casts its fishing-net into the branches.
The urn of light
sinks into the sea.
Shadows anchor out in the bay.

They come back, swimming through mist,
saturated
with the reed-haze of Brandenburg meadows,
the Wendish willow mothers,
the warty old women
with gaping breasts,
at the margins of pools,
the sealed-in, dark-eyed water,
their feet thrust deep into the earth,
this is what I remember.

The Potters' Island

Behind us the icy bird
with white wings,
the snow-wind,
the drenched sail
impressed on the water.

Die Töpferinsel,
der unergründliche Fels,
wo tote Tage in den Kammern
zerbrochener Öfen brennen.
Die Lasur der Schmerzen
schimmert in großer Kälte.

Mit dem Druck der Hand
gaben sie dem feuchten Ton
auf kreisender Scheibe
die Wölbung
der Urnen und Amphoren.

Später rieben sie Farben,
Kienruß, Ocker und Kreide,
brannten den Vasen
gemalte Zeichen ein.
Sie fuhren aus, um Handel
an den Küsten zu treiben.

Ein spitzer Rattenschädel
liegt zwischen Scherben
und schwarzer Spreu.
Im Bottich Asche,
splittrige Knochen.
Wir segeln vorbei.

Die Armut des Heiligen

Wer du auch seist,
geheiligtes Gebein,
bleckender Kiefer,
unter den Rippenbogen,
mit Golddraht umwickelt,
brannte ein Herz.

The potters' island,
inscrutable cliffs,
where dead days burn
in corners of broken kilns.
Glaze of hardship
shining in a great cold.

With the press of a hand
at the turning wheel,
they gave wet clay
the curvature
of amphorae and urns.

Later they daubed colour,
ochre, lampblack, chalk,
firing the vases
to give each its mark.
They struck out, trading
along the coast.

Sharps of a rat skull
lie between shards
and blackened chaff.
Ashes in a barrel,
splintered bones.
And we sail on.

Poverty of the Holy

Whoever you are,
hallowed bones,
flayed jawbone,
under the rib-cage,
swathed in golden wire,
burned a heart.

Wenn der Frost
die Steine hebt,
spricht das Gnadenlose
das Lob der Schöpfung.

Auf den Tod von V. W.

Sie vergaß die Asche
auf den gekrümmten Tasten des Klaviers,
das flackernde Licht in den Fenstern.

Mit einem Teich begann es,
dann kam der steinige Weg,
der umgitterte Brunnen, von Beifuß bewachsen,
die löchrige Tränke unter der Ulme,
wo einst die Pferde standen.

Dann kam die Nacht,
die wie ein fallendes Wasser war.
Manchmal, für Stunden,
ein Vogelgeist,
halb Bussard, halb Schwan,
hart über dem Schilf,
aus dem ein Schneesturm heult.

Achtwegewinkel

Achtwegewinkel,
zartknochig liegt die Amsel
im Sand,
die Krallen in die Luft gespreizt.
Aus grauem Nebel rinnt
der Schnee

When the frost
heaves at stones,
the merciless utters
in praise of creation.

On the Death of V. W.

She forgot the ash
on the warped piano keys,
the flickering of light at the window.

It began with a pond,
then came the rocky path,
the fenced-off well, overgrown with mugwort,
the leaking water-trough beneath the elm,
where horses once stood.

Then came night,
more like the falling of water.
Sometimes, for hours,
a bird-spirit,
half buzzard, half swan,
steadfast above the reeds,
out of which a snow-storm howls.

Where Eight Ways Meet

Where eight ways meet,
the delicate-boned blackbird lies
in the sand,
its claws spread to the air.
Out of a grey fog
snow flooding

ins brüchige Röhricht
des Tümpels.

Wer hat die Finsternis angesiedelt?
Wer hat das Schweigen vermauert mit Steinen,
den Kalk mit Galle gemischt?

Achtwegewinkel,
es steht geschrieben,
versiegelt
mit dem Brandmal des Widders:
Die beuligen Stämme
der Weiden werden sich krümmen
und Asche sein, wenn einst
auf schartigen Füßen
die Boten im Feuer
verlassen die Stadt.

M. V.

Er ging fort,
das Zimmer ist leer,
der Ofen kalt,
die Flaschen recken die Hälse.
Er ließ nichts zurück
als eine Fußspur im Sand,
vom Eis des Winters ausgegossen.

Der Sturm der Chaussee
begrub ihn nachts.
Hinsinkend
ins starre Schneegesträuch,
fand er den Schlüssel,
der ihm die Türen öffnet.

into the brittle reed-beds
of the ponds.

Who established the darkness?
Who walled up silence in stone,
mixed bile with lime?

Where eight ways meet,
it is written,
sealed
with the sign of Aries:
bulbous trunks
of willow trees will bend
and become ash, when once
on their ragged legs
the messengers of fire
leave the city.

M. V.

He vanished—
the room is empty,
the oven cold,
the bottles crane their necks.
He left nothing behind
as if a footprint in sand,
a spill of ice in winter.

The highway storm
buried him at night.
Sinking down
into bushes stiff with snow,
he found the key
that opens doors for him.

Vor Nîmes 1452

I

Oktober, November,
die Lungen des Herbstes
atmen die Nebel aus.
Im düsteren Licht
das flüchtende Grau der Rehe.

Steck deine Klinge ein,
ruchloser Gast,
setz dich ans Feuer,
misch deine Karten.

Kreuz-As, gezinkt
mit einer Spur
verharschten Bluts.
Im düsteren Licht
das flüchtende Grau der Rehe.

II

Ich rief hinauf:
Laudetur, Jesu-Christ,
und hob die frostverbrannte Faust.

Der Müller starrte aus der Luke,
er sah den Mond,
den grauen Mahlstein.

Leer rasselt
die Ginsterschote
im Mahlgang der Sterne.

Dezemberrissiges Eichenlaub,
kümmerndes Birkengestrüpp,
Zunder genug, ein Feuer zu machen.

Before Nîmes 1452

I

October, November,
the lungs of autumn
breathe out fog.
In the dim light
the fleet grey of deer.

Sheathe your sword,
pitiless guest,
sit beside the fire,
shuffle your cards.

The ace of clubs,
stained with a trace
of crusted blood.
In the dim light
the fleet grey of deer.

II

I called out:
Laudetur, Jesu-Christ,
and raised a frost-burned fist.

The miller stared from his skylight,
he glimpsed the moon,
a grey millstone.

The gorse pods'
hollow rattling
under the grinding of the stars.

December-dry oak leaves,
shrivelled birch scrub,
here's tinder enough to catch a fire.

Leicht ist bei frischem Schnee
am Hühnerstall
die schnurgrade Spur
des Fuchses zu finden.

III

Unglück,
mein Bruder
in schneeloser Kälte.

Über dem Wald
neun schwarze Punkte
im blassen Fleisch des Winterhimmels.

Sind es die Jahre,
dir zugemessen?

Sind es die Krähen,
die langsam näher kommen,
dich zu zerfleischen?

In the fall of fresh snow
beside the hen coop,
easy to find the straight path
of the foxes.

III

Disaster,
my brother
in the snowless chill.

Above the wood
nine black specks
in the pale flesh of the winter sky.

Are these the years
assigned to you?

Are these the crows
that are coming slowly closer
to tear you to pieces?

III

III

Winter

Das kalte Eisen des Dezembers
hallt am Pfahl,
mit harter Faust
vom Wind geschlagen.
Die Fähre eingefroren.
Fischkästen, bereift,
von Möwen bevölkert.

Am blätterdunstigen Feuer,
die Pelzmütze
tief über die Ohren gezogen,
hocken fremde Soldaten.

In dünnen zerfransten Mänteln
Gefangene
um eine Eiche geschart.
Sie blicken zum Fluß.
Zwei Frauen
in schneeverkrusteten Schaffelljacken
gehen nach Norden
über das Eis.

Die Niederlage

I

In der Kälte des Nordwinds
lag ich auf Jutesäcken
unter der Laderampe des Güterbahnhofs.
Der Wechsel von Schüssen und dichter Stille.
An der Wand
wie immer am Abend
das Gewebe aus Licht und Dämmerung.
Zwischen den Gleisen
rupfte ein Rind mit rauher Zunge
das rostig braune Gras.

Winter

The cold iron of December
clangs at the stake,
lashed by the brutal fist
of the wind.
The ferry's ice-bound.
Fish-crates, hoar-frosted,
mobbed by gulls.

At their leaf-smoking fire,
fur hats
pulled down over their ears,
squat foreign soldiers.

In thin and fraying coats
prisoners
gathered round an oak.
They look across the river.
Two women
in snow-encrusted sheepskin jackets
head north
across the ice.

Defeat

I

In the freeze of the north wind
I lay on gunny sacks
under the loading ramp at the freight station.
Alternating gunfire and fraught silence.
On the wall
as always come evening,
a weave of light and dusk.
Between the tracks
a cow pulled at rusty-brown grass
with its rough tongue.

II

Überquerend die Schienen,
war ich in dünner Sonne
nicht mehr als der frierende Schatten,
der vor mir ging.
Auf der Brache
erdige Klumpen,
Tote in harschigen Mänteln.
In Fußlappen einer,
er starrte
durch blutverkrustete Finger
das Eisengerippe der Schranke an.

III

Am Eingang des Dorfs warf der Wind
eine geballte Ladung Frost
gegen die Mauer.
Der Mond legte fasrige Gaze
über die Wunden der Dächer.

Langsam sank die Leere der Nacht
und füllte sich mit Hundegeheul.
Es sank die Niederlage
auf die gefrorenen Adern des Landes
und auf die ledergepolsterten Sitze
des alten Kremsers in der Remise,
wo zwischen Pferdegeschirr und grauem Heu
die Kinder schliefen.
Sie sank auf die blaugefleckte Haut der Toten,
die Steine und Bäume umarmten.

II

Across the rails,
I moved into a watery sunlight
no more than the freezing shadow
that ran before me.
On the fallow
lumps of earth,
the dead in their brutal clothing.
With rag-bound feet,
he stared
through blood-encrusted knuckles
towards the iron-ribbed barrier crossing.

III

At the edge of the village the wind
flung its ton of frost
against the wall.
The moon lowered a fibrous gauze
on the wounds of the rooftops.

Slowly the emptiness of night descended,
filled with the howling of dogs.
Defeat sank
into the frozen veins of the country,
into the leather-upholstered seats
of old Kremsers in the coach sheds,
between the horse tack and grey straw
where children slept.
It sank into the blue-blotched skin of the dead,
their embrace of rocks and trees.

Der Schlammfang

Eines Abends kamen
aus einem Loch im Asphalt
Männer mit Masken.
Sie rochen nach seifigem Schlamm,
im Netzwerk trug einer
tote Fische
und grüne Wasserratten.
Abwässer liefen von ihren Stiefeln.
Niemand wollte sie sehen
in der Stadt,
jeder schloß die Tür.
Sie zogen über den Markt und schwanden
im Gebüsch verkohlter Schrebergärten.
Eine schillernde Muschel
hing einem im Haar.
Noch lange glomm sie
im öligen Spiegel der Straße.

Middleham Castle

Vertraut mit den Gewohnheiten großer Wälder,
das Jahr streift in den Farben des Eichelhähers
die schmerzliche Helle erstarrter Äste,
das Winterhaar des Hirsches klebt an der Rinde,
die Kälber stehen abends dicht gedrängt,
sich wärmend an der Wolke des eigenen Atems,
zieh ich mit Stricken und Pferden die Stämme
den Ginsterhügel hinauf nach Middleham Castle.

Dies will ich bezeugen, beim Herdfeuer hier.
Im Mond sah ich den hinkenden Schatten
des Königs, Gloster ging um, in Rot gekleidet,
den schmutzigen Zobel über dem Buckel,
das kurze Schwert am Gürtel. Er kroch

Mudtrappers

One evening out of a hole
in the asphalt
men in masks appeared.
They stank of a soapy sludge,
one carried dead fish
in netting
and green water-rats.
Sewage spilled from their boots.
No-one wished to see them
across town,
everyone shutting their doors.
They swarmed over the market place and vanished
into the scrub of a burnt-out allotment.
An iridescent mussel shell
snagged in the hair of one of them.
For ages it lay there, gleaming
in the street's greasy mirror.

Middleham Castle

Familiar with the ways of great forests—
the year streaked with jays' colours,
the painful brightness of frosted boughs,
winter hair of deer stuck to bark,
fawns huddled together in the evening,
warming themselves in the cloud of their breathing—
up the gorse-clad hill with ropes and horses
I haul tree trunks to Middleham Castle.

Here at the fireside, I swear to this.
By moonlight I saw the limping shadow
of the king, Gloucester walked there, clad in red,
a filthy sable across his hump,
a dagger at his belt. He crawled

durch mächtige Wurzeln der Eiche in die Erde.
Dort lag ein Klumpen geronnenen Bluts,
aus dem er Ketten und Ringe zerrte.

In Nächten langer Helle
steht er im brüchigen Schatten
des Faulbaums an der Mauer,
die weißen Schwalben
nisten in seinem Zimmer.

Er stieg aus seiner Grube,
gräserstill,
die Wolfsmilch ätzte seine Spur.
Hornissen schwärmten,
der Überfall von Blüten
konnt ihn nicht ersticken.

Wurmstichig ist sein Fuß.
Die Steine schleifend,
geht Gloster zu den Ställen.
Die Doggen senken ihren Kopf
dem Peitschenhieb entgegen.

Knechte sind wir
und fürchten sein Messer,
liegt auch sein Schädel,
von vielen Wintern kahlgepickt,
tief in der Erde.

into the ground through huge roots of oak.
A mass of congealed blood lay there
from which he pulled rings and chains.

In night's long brightness
he stands in the broken shadows
of alder buckthorn by the wall;
white swallows build nests
in his room.

He rose from his hollow,
silent as grass,
milkweed etched his trail.
Hornets swarmed;
the assault of blossoms
could not choke him.

His foot is worm-eaten.
Scraping the flagstones,
Gloucester walks to the stables.
The mastiffs lower their heads
anticipating the whip.

We are his servants,
we go in fear of his blade,
though his skull,
picked clean by so many winters,
lies deep in the ground.

Macbeth

Mit Hexen redete ich,
in welcher Sprache,
ich weiß es nicht mehr.

Aufgesprengt
die Tore des Himmels,
freigelassen der Geist,
in Windwirbeln
das Gelichter der Heide.

Am Meer
die schmutzigen Zehen des Schnees,
hier wartet einer
mit Händen ohne Haut.
Ich wollt, meine Mutter
hätt mich erstickt.

Aus den Ställen des Winds
wird er kommen,
wo die alten Frauen
das Futter häckseln.

Argwohn mein Helm,
ich häng ihn
ins Gebälk der Nacht.

Alter Kupferstich

Der dünne Staub
im Uhrengehäuse
meldet die Ankunft des Todes.

Noch geht der Perpendikel,
er schwingt den Bruchteil eines Kreises.
Der Tod verlangt den ganzen Kreis.

Macbeth

I spoke with the witches,
in what language
I don't remember.

Blown open,
the gates of heaven,
unleashed the spirit
in whirlwinds,
the rabble of the heath.

Down to the sea
the filthy toes of the snow,
one waiting here
hands flayed.
My wish—that my mother
had stifled me.

He will come
from the stalls of the wind,
where the old women
shred fodder.

My helmet, mistrust,
I let it hang
in the rafters of night.

Old Copperplate

A thin dusting
on the clock case
announces the advent of death.

Yet the pendulum moves,
swinging a fraction of a circle.
Death demands the whole circle.

Ein Fräulein am Fenster
im Gewitterwind.
Fünf Rosenblätter wehn durchs Zimmer.

Der Blitz gibt einer Sekunde Macht.
Die hetzenden Pferde,
der schwarzen Kutsche vorgespannt,
sind schneller.

Die Nüstern
brennen im Spiegel.
Oder sind es die Kerzen,
die außerhalb des Rahmens
in hohen Leuchtern stehn?

Odysseus und die Circe

Mit einem Topf,
von Feuer berußt,
das reine Wasser aus dem Bach
zu schöpfen,
ist eine Kunst.
Nimm doch den Helm ab,
Odysseus.

So höhnte die Stimme
der Circe in heißer Luft.
Ich nahm den Helm ab,
da war kein Wasser.

Ich lag in der Hitze
verbrannten Grases,
den Gaumen trocken,
die Haut riß
über den Backenknochen.

At the window, a girl
in a thunderstorm.
Five rose petals fly across the room.

Lightning lends power to the instant.
The roused horses,
harnessed to the black coach,
but outrunning it.

Their nostrils
incandescent in the mirror.
Or just candles,
beyond the edge of the frame
standing tall in their candelabra?

Odysseus and Circe

With a pan,
soot-blackened in the fire,
to scoop out
pure water from a stream—
that's an art.
Why not take off your helmet,
Odysseus.

The voice of Circe mocked
in the burning air.
I removed my helmet,
but no sign of water.

I lay in the wavering heat
of the scorched grasses,
my throat parched,
skin peeling
from the bones of my cheeks.

Am Mittag,
bei heller Stirn der Berge,
die enge Schlucht. Ich stieg hinab,
den Felsenschutt im Nacken,
Steine fielen
an meinem Kopf vorbei.

Ausgesetzt der hallenden Öde,
hörte ich die Mittagsstimme:
Wenn du im Herzen
die Wahrheit bewegst,
die Lüge bewegst,
die List,
erschlagen dich die Steine.

Eingeklemmt
in narbigen Fels,
mit nassem Rücken,
die Knöchel zerschunden,
schmeckte ich die grillige Stimme
und sah im Dunst des Steinschlags
die Augen einer Quelle.

Undine

Mit dem Jahr wächst das Schilf
und die bräunlichen Kolben
brechen wollig auf.

Der Fischer, der morgens
durchs Wasser watet,
schiebt den teerigen Kahn
an meiner Schulter vorbei.

Eine Legende bin ich,
ein Wasser grau bewegt,

By midday,
on the shining brow of the peaks,
a narrow valley. I descended,
rock-falls about my shoulders,
stones tumbling
around my head.

Exposed in that echoing wasteland,
I heard the voice of noon:
if in your heart
you shift the truth,
dislodge the lie,
the guile,
the stones will destroy you.

Pinned down
on that scarred rockface,
my back drenched,
ankles black and blue,
I tasted that surly voice
and through the haze of rock-falls
saw the wink of a spring.

Undine

With the year, reeds grow tall
and their brown pistons
burst with wool.

Wading water in the morning,
the fisherman hauling
his tarry-bottomed punt along
across my shoulder.

I am a legend,
a grey eddy of water,

in dem die Reusen
und Blätter schwimmen.

In Wurzelkörben
unterwaschener Weiden
schwankt mit dem Laich
der Fische mein Schmuck,
vom Maul der Hechte bewacht.

Wenn die Libellen
im Sommer das Licht vergittern,
das unbewegliche Licht
von Rohr und Wasser,
lieg ich im Kerker des Sees.

Die Rohrdommel steht,
ein Weidenpfahl,
im sickernden Grün der Algen.
Und hinter Nebelwolken der Mond,
eine graue Hornissenwabe.

Am Jordan

Söhne,
hebt mich auf,
hebt mich ins große Vergessen,
in den Rauch, der nichts verdunkelt,
in die flammende Akazie,
niederstürzend über dem Wind,
in den Steppenhimmel
wandernder Schafe.

An diesem Morgen
bewundern meine eitrigen Augen,
die Hagar sahen,
den fließenden Schimmer
des Jordans
auf bleibenden Weidenblättern.

swimming among
the leaves and fish-traps.

In the freshly-flushed baskets
of willow roots,
swaying with the spawn
of fish, my jewellery,
in the safe-keeping of pikes' jaws.

As dragonflies
criss-cross the light of summer,
the unmoving light
of reed-bed and water,
I languish in the prison of the lake.

The bittern stands,
a willow stump,
in the green ooze of algae.
And beyond the fogbanks of the moon,
the hornets' grey honeycomb.

Beside Jordan

Sons,
raise me up,
lift me into the great forgetting,
into smoke, that dims nothing,
into the blazing acacia
tumbling in the wind,
onto the downland heaven
of migrating sheep.

This morning,
my suppurating eyes,
that saw Hagar,
marvel at the fluent glittering
of Jordan
on the last of the willow leaves.

Alt-Seidenberg

Vieh hütend
zu Füßen der großen Späherin,
der Landschaft mit Krähe und Pappel,
sah er über der Stadt
die glasige Kugel des Äthers,
er hörte Stimmen in den Lüften,
Posaunenstöße, hell und schneidend,
Geräusche hinter den Uferweiden,
das Waschen und Scheren der Schafe.

Am Mittag
fand er im Hügel eine Höhle
von Wurzeln starrend,
im Winkelmaß der Schatten
stak eine Bütte Gold.
Er wich zurück und schlug
das spukabwehrende Zeichen,
Reiter
auf Pferden mit fleischigen Mähnen
ritten an Gruben
voll Haar und Blut vorbei.

Anderen Tages
war es wie immer,
verschlossen die Erde,
mit Feldspat versiegelt.
Nur eine Hummel summte dort,
vom Wind ins dürre Gras gedrückt.

Das Feuer,
das in der Einöde brannte,
stieg in die Höhe,
das Wasser strömte der Tiefe zu.
Die Spuren der Herde führten zur Tränke.
Der Hügel trug den Himmel
auf steinigem Nacken.

Alt-Seidenberg

Tending cattle
at the foot of the high scout-rock,
a landscape of crow and poplar tree,
above the town he saw
the glassy sphere of the ether,
heard voices on the air,
trumpet-blasts, bright and shrill,
sounds far beyond the river meadow,
the dipping and shearing of sheep.

At midday
in the hills he discovered a cave
barely glimpsed between roots—
in the twisted mass of shadows
lay a crock of gold.
He backed away, he made
the sign to ward off spirits,
riders
on horses with fleshy manes
rode through pits
brimming with blood and hair.

On other days
it was as always,
the earth shut tight,
sealed with feldspar.
Only a bumble bee buzzing there,
pressed by the wind into the parched grass.

The fire,
set burning in the desert,
rose to such a height,
water poured into the deep.
The tracks of the herd led to the drinking troughs.
The hillside bore the sky
round its stony neck.

IV

IV

Die Nachbarn

Für Hermann Kesten

Die Ruhe des Stroms,
das Feuer der Erde,
die leere Finsternis des Himmels
sind meine gefährlichen Nachbarn.

Der Reiher kann sich von vielen Seen
das seichte schilfige Wasser wählen,
wo er mit jähem Stoß
die Beute greift und tötet.

Nicht kann das Wasser
den Reiher wählen.
Geduldig trägt es die Furcht der Fische,
den heiseren Schrei des hungrigen Vogels.

Wasser und Reiher,
beide sind Nachbarn
von hohen Erlen,
von Rohr und Fröschen.

Geknetet in Gleichmut,
essen die Menschen, meine Nachbarn,
täglich ihr Brot.
Keiner will Asche sein.

Keinem gelingt es,
die Münze zu prägen,
die noch gilt
in eisiger Nacht.

Neighbours

for Hermann Kesten

The calm of the stream,
the fire of the earth,
empty darkness of sky,
are my dangerous neighbours.

The heron chooses from many lakes
the reedy shallow reaches
where with a sudden stab
it strikes and kills its prey.

The water's not able
to choose its heron.
Patiently it bears the fright of fishes,
harsh cry of the ravenous bird.

Water and heron—
both are neighbours
to tall alders,
to frogs and reeds.

Kneaded to composure,
men and women, my neighbours,
consume their daily bread.
Nobody wants to be ash.

Nobody succeeds
in striking a coin
that passes for legal tender
in the icy night.

Keine Antwort

Aufs schwimmende Nebelhaupt
der Eiche
setzt sich die Krähe.
Der Katzenbalken ist leer.

Schatten von dürrem
Weingerank
an der Zimmerdecke.
Zeichen,
von eines Mandarinen Hand
geschrieben.

Das Alphabet,
das du besitzt,
reicht nicht aus,
Antwort zu geben
der wehrlosen Schrift.

Auf der Strasse Nach Viznar

Die Nacht erlosch
in öliger Blindheit des Lampenglases,
der dünne Faden blakenden Rauchs
sank auf den Docht zurück.
Wir spähten ins Zwielicht.

Sie sprangen vom Wagen
und trieben die Gefesselten
ins schläfernde Grau,
das später heller wurde über den Gewehren.

Sie töten
in der klaren Frühe des Taus.

No Answer

Up through swimming fog
an oak tree,
a crow perched in it.
The cats' post deserted.

Shadows of withered
vines
across the ceiling.
Signs,
written by the hand
of a Mandarin.

The alphabet,
in your possession,
it's not good enough—
no answer
to the helpless script.

On the Road to Viznar

Night vanishing
into the greasy blindness of lamp-glasses,
a thin thread of sooty smoke
slumps to the wick.
We peer out into the half-light.

They leaped from a wagon
and drove the shackled men
into the sleepy grey,
growing brighter later with their guns.

They kill
in the clear dew of dawn.

November

November
schläft in der Öde
gerodeten Bodens,
sumpfiges Licht und
Fäulnis eines Rohrgewässers,
in dem die Sichel nicht mehr blinkt.

Kein Himmel
reißt in Feuern auf,
wo die Gefangenen liegen
am Wasser Chebar.

Die Esel tragen
den Nebel in die Stadt.
Die Pinien
säen Finsternis.

Schnee
Dem Gedächtnis Hans Henny Jahnns

Der Schnee treibt,
das große Schleppnetz des Himmels,
es wird die Toten nicht fangen.

Der Schnee wechselt
sein Lager.
Er stäubt von Ast zu Ast.

Die blauen Schatten
der Füchse lauern
im Hinterhalt. Sie wittern

die weiße
Kehle der Einsamkeit.

November

November
slumbers in the waste
of scoured ground,
swamp-light and
the rot of reedy water reaches
where the scythe no longer flashes.

No heaven
bursts open in flames
where the captives lie
beside the River Chebar.

The donkeys lug
fog into town.
The pines
seed darkness.

Snow
in memory of Hans Henny Jahnn

The snow drives on,
the great drag-net of the heavens—
it will not catch the dead.

Snow shifts
camp.
It skips from branch to branch.

The blue shadows
of foxes lie
in wait. They scent

the white
throat of the solitary.

Die Engel

Ein Rauch,
ein Schatten steht auf,
geht durch das Zimmer,
wo eine Greisin,
den Gänseflügel
in schwacher Hand,
den Sims des Ofens fegt.
Ein Feuer brennt.
Gedenke meiner,
flüstert der Staub.

Novembernebel, Regen, Regen
und Katzenschlaf.
Der Himmel schwarz
und schlammig über dem Fluß.
Aus klaffender Leere fließt die Zeit,
fließt über die Flossen
und Kiemen der Fische
und über die eisigen Augen
der Engel,
die niederfahren hinter der dünnen Dämmerung,
mit rußigen Schwingen zu den Töchtern Kains.

Ein Rauch,
ein Schatten steht auf,
geht durch das Zimmer.
Ein Feuer brennt.
Gedenke meiner,
flüstert der Staub.

The Angels

A smoky fume,
a shadow rises,
crossing the room
where an old woman,
with a goose's wing
in her feeble hand,
brushes the edge of the stove.
A fire burns.
Remember me,
whispers the dust.

November fog, the rain, the rain
and the somnolence of cats.
The sky is black
and muddy above the river.
Time pours from a gaping emptiness,
pours over the fins
and gills of fish
and over the icy eyes
of the angels,
descended beyond the feeble dusk,
on sooty wings to the daughters of Cain.

A smoky fume,
a shadow rises,
crossing the room.
A fire burns.
Remember me,
whispers the dust.

Aristeas

Die erste Frühe,
als im Gewölk das Gold
der Toten lag. Es schlief der Wind,
wo im Geäst
die nebelgefiederte Krähe saß.

Der Vogel flog,
sein Fittich schlug das Licht
im Erlengrau,
die milchige Haut der Steppe.

Ich, Aristeas,
als Krähe einem Gott gefolgt,
ich schweife,
vom Traum gerissen,
durch Lorbeerhaine des Nebels,
mit starrem Flügel den Morgen suchend.
Ich spähte
in schneeverkrustete Höhlen,
Gesichter, einäugig, feuerbeschienen,
versanken im Rauch.
Und Pferde standen, vereist die Mähnen,
an Pflöcke gefesselt mit Riemen aus Ruß.

Die Krähe strich
ins winterliche Tor,
strich durch verhungertes Gesträuch.
Frost stäubte auf.
Und eine dürre Zunge sprach:
Hier ist das Vergangene ohne Schmerz.

Aristeas

The dawn light—
like the gilding of the dead
it lay on the clouds. The wind slept,
among branches there sat
the fog-befeathered crow.

The bird flew,
its wings beating the light
in the alders' grey,
the milky pelt of the downs.

    I, Aristeas,
    who in the shape of a crow pursued a god,
    I wander,
    torn from a dream,
    through laurel groves of mist,
    with stiff wings in search of morning.
    I peered
    into snow-encrusted caves,
    faces, one-eyed, fire-lit,
    vanished into smoke.
    And horses, frost-maned, stood
    tethered to stakes by sooty bridles.

The crow swept
through a wintry gate,
swept through starved undergrowth.
The frost danced.
A parched tongue spoke:
here what is past is without pain.

Delphine

Meerwärts spähend
bei weißer Sonne
ich seh sie springen
aus der salzigen
Schwere des Wassers –
Delphine,

meine heimlichen Brüder,
tragen die Botschaft
nach Byzanz.

Es knistert die Luft,
als flöge feuriges Stroh
durch Tamariskenbüsche.

Hier will ich bleiben
und zählen am Hang,
wolfgraue Schlucht,
die schmalen hohen
Steine,
schartig vom Grillengewetz,
die Steine der Toten,
von Mittagshimmeln geschwärzt.

Der Kundschafter

Wir lagen in Kratern,
in brandigen Löchern
des Sündenfalls.
Die magere Füchsin
wärmte den Teich aus Geröll.

Aufrecht,
auf dem Schatten eines Baums,

Dolphins

Gazing out across the sea
in white sunlight
I saw them leap
above the salty
weight of the water—
dolphins,

my secret brothers,
carrying my messages
to Byzantium.

Here a crackle in the air,
as of flying, fiery straw
through the tamarisk bushes.

I will remain here
to count on the hillside,
the wolf-grey gorge,
high narrow
stones,
cricket-honed to a jagged edge,
stones of the dead,
blackened under noon skies.

The Scout

We sprawled in craters,
in fire holes
of man's falling.
The skinny vixen
warms the rubble-strewn pool.

Erect,
from the trees' shadows,

setzte er über den Strom,
das Land verlassend, die grobe Öde,
wo Frost die Steine sprengt
mit blankem Keil.

Wir sahen ihn treiben
unter schneelosem Himmel
in die Dämmerung hinein,
bis eine Nebelwand
ihn zögernd aufnahm,
eine Höhle, bewohnbar.

Abschied von den Hirten

Nun da du gehst
vergiß die felsenkühle Nacht,
vergiß die Hirten,
sie bogen dem Widder den Hals zurück
und eine graubehaarte Hand
stieß ihm das Messer in die Kehle.

Im Nebelgewoge
schwimmt wieder das Licht
der ersten Schöpfung. Und unter der Tanne
der nicht zu Ende
geschlagene Kreis aus Nadeln und Nässe.
Dies ist dein Zeichen. Vergiß die Hirten.

he moved across the stream,
leaving the country, the rough wilderness,
where frost splinters stones
with its gleaming wedge.

We watched him push on
beneath a snowless sky
into the twilight,
till a wall of fog
took him hesitantly in,
a cave, a place to live in.

Farewell to Shepherds

And now you are leaving,
forget the mountain-cool night,
forget the shepherds—
they twisted back the ram's neck
and a hairy, grey hand
thrust the knife into its throat.

On foggy billows
the light of first creation
swims back. And beneath the pine tree,
left incomplete,
the trampled circle of damp and needles.
This is your sign. Forget the shepherds.

Jeden Abend

Jeden Abend
wenn im Steinbruch das letzte Signal
wie eine Klage verweht,
geh ich unter der weiten Bläue des Oktoberhimmels
über die Wiesen zum Fluß hinunter
am Neubau vorbei.

Ein mürrischer Mann,
gestützt auf seine Kohlenforke,
starrt in die zuckende Glut des Koks,
die hinter den Rippen der Eisenkörbe
gefangen lebt.
Er bewacht das Feuer.
Die Wasserratte, raschelnd im Schilf,
bewacht die sinkende Dämmerung.

Die Kreatur

Das Brennglas dünnen Eises,
das morgens im Eimer schwimmt,
zeigt den Stand der Sonne an.

Ein Mann in abgeschabter Jacke
zieht auf dem Hof
im müden Kreis
die Maultierstute hinter sich her,
das Fell vom Kummet wundgestoßen.

Sie lahmt, als läge
ein Stein unter dem lockeren Eisen
des linken Hinterhufs.
Es näßt der Fesselbehang.

Every Evening

Every evening,
when the last siren is sounding from the quarry
like a scattered wailing,
I walk under the broad, blue October skies
across the meadows down to the river
beside the new building site.

A sullen man,
propped on his coal shovel,
gazes at the flickering embers of coal,
barely alight
behind the ribs of the iron brazier.
He looks to the fire.
The water-rat, scuttling in the reeds,
looks to the fall of twilight.

The Creature

The flaming lens of thin ice,
where it floats in the morning pail,
marks the height of the sun.

A man in a threadbare jacket
is about the yard
dragging the mule behind him
in a tired circle,
her pelt rubbed sore beneath the harness.

She's lame, most likely
a stone lodged under the loosened shoe
of her left rear hoof.
The fetlock oozes.

Mit einem Strohwisch
die Flanke des Tieres reibend,
starrt er mit schweißig leerem
Gesicht die Berge an.
Er sieht den Hafer in der Kiste,
dumpf und schimmlig,
von Pilzen befallen.
Er sieht die Stute mit schlechtem Gebiß,
die Hungergrube in den Wolken.

An der rußigen Mauer
der Abdeckerei
neigt sich die Sonne zur Unterwelt.

Unter der blanken Hacke des Monds

Unter der blanken Hacke des Monds
werde ich sterben,
ohne das Alphabet der Blitze
gelernt zu haben.

Im Wasserzeichen der Nacht
die Kindheit der Mythen,
nicht zu entziffern.

Unwissend
stürz ich hinab,
zu den Knochen der Füchse geworfen.

With a handful of straw,
rubbing at the animal's flank,
he gazes with a vacant, sweating face
towards the mountains.
He sees oats in the tub,
mildewed and mouldy,
full of fungus.
He sees the mare with her rotten teeth,
starved hollows of the clouds.

At the sooty wall
of the knacker's yard
the sun tilts towards the underworld.

Under the Shining Blade of the Moon

Under the shining blade of the moon
is where I'll die,
without having learned
the alphabet of lightning.

Deep in night's watermark
the infancy of myths,
indecipherable.

Ignorant,
I fall headlong,
flung to the bones of foxes.

v

v

Gehölz

Für Heinrich Böll

Gehölz
habichtsgrau,
das Grillenlicht der Mittagsdürre,
dahinter das Haus,
gebaut auf eine Wasserader.

Wasser,
verborgen,
in sandiger Öde,
du strömtest in den Durst der Sprache,
du zogst die Blitze an.

Am Eingang der Erde,
sagt eine Stimme, wo Steine
und Wurzeln die Tür verriegeln,
sind die zerwühlten Knochen Hiobs
zu Sand geworden, dort steht noch
sein Napf voll Regenwasser.

Im Gouvernement W.

Keine Nachricht.
Mit blanken Zangen kappt
der Frost den Draht der Telegrafenmasten.
Schneepflüge, Eisenflossen räumen
die Kälte nicht fort.

Taubstumme Boten
besuchen dich nachts.
Sie treten über die Schwelle,
das Stroh von den Stiefeln schleudernd,
noch warm
vom angeheizten Ziegelstein
im Schlittenkasten.

Copse

for Heinrich Böll

A copse,
hawk-grey,
the cricket-glinting of midday drought—
beyond it the house,
built on a vein of water.

Water,
obscured,
in the sandy wasteland,
you poured into the thirst for speech,
you drew lightning.

At the earth's opening,
a voice speaks, where the door is barred
by roots and stones,
the churned-up bones
of Job turned to sand—there still
his bowl of rainwater stands.

In W. District

No news.
With its glittering pliers
frost cuts the wires on telegraph poles.
Snowploughs, their iron blades
unable to shift the cold.

Deaf-mute messengers
visit you by night.
They burst across the threshold,
kicking straw from their boots
still warm
from the heated bricks
in their sledges.

Sie lachen lautlos
und stechen mit eisernen Griffeln
die Namen der Opfer
in die Schläfe der Luft.

Alkaios

Die Spur verlischt. Es richtet
sich auf das Gras
wie eine Wahrheit. Während du gehst,
koppelt der ummauerte Hof
die Hunde los. Hier ist der Weg,
von Winterwassern
ins Gestrüpp gehauen.

Und unten, zwischen den Felsenzähnen,
die Mühsal des Meeres, die Brandung,
zerbrochene Ruder, das Nichts
auf den Strand zu schleudern.

Sie haben
mit eisernen Pfählen
die Grenze gesetzt. Noch wehrt
sich der Tag mit seinen Disteln
gegen den eisigen
Anschlag der Nacht.

They laugh noiselessly
and with an iron pencil
stab the names of their victims
into the temple of the air.

Alkaios

The track gives out. It points
off into the grass
like a truth. As you pass by,
the walled yard lets
loose its dogs. Here's the path—
scoured through scrubland
by winter's run off.

And below, between the rocks' teeth,
the toiling of the sea, surge,
smashed rudder, the nothingness
cast up onto the beach.

They have
staked out the border
with iron posts. Day still
defends itself with its thistles
even against the icy
onslaught of night.

Die Reise

Für Marie Luise Kaschnitz

Eines Abends
im späten November flacher Seen
trat aus dem Regengeräusch ein Mann.
Wir nahmen den Pfad durchs hohe Rohr.
Es wehte kühl an meine Schläfen,
als ging ich
zwischen den Mähnen zweier Pferde.
Sie trugen
in Säcken aus Nebel
mein Gepäck,
das leichter war als der Nachtwind
über dem Schilf.

Nicht der Fährtenkundige,
der noch im Geröll
das Wasser und die Taube findet,
der Schwache
mit schwärender Schulter führte mich,
wo an den Pfählen
der weiße Rauch
ins Dickicht eiserner Disteln zog.

Die Ordnung der Gewitter

Die verbissene Ordnung der Gewitter,
eines zieht herauf
von den südlichen Havelseen,
schlagend eine wüste Schneise
durch Dörfer und Wälder,
das andere zögert, am Wind sich stauend,
stürzt jäh mit heftigen Hagelschauern
über die Hügel von Saarmund.
Beide treffen über meinem Dach zusammen.

The Journey

for Marie Luise Kaschnitz

One evening
among the flat lakes of late November,
a man stepped out from the beat of the rain.
We took the path through tall reeds.
They slid cool across my temples,
as if I travelled
between the manes of two horses.
They carried,
in satchels of mist,
my luggage
that was lighter than the night breeze
across the reeds.

Not the skilled path-finder,
still able to track
the water and the dove in the debris—
the feeble one
with the festering shoulder led me,
where among the stakes
white smoke withdrew
into thickets of iron-hard thistles.

The Order of the Storm

The grim order of the storm—
one coming
from south of the Havel lakes,
cutting a desolate path
through villages and woods,
the other hesitating, wind gathering,
abruptly crashes with violent hailstorms
over the Saarmund hills.
Both collide above my roof.

Die Posaunen verscharrt
in finsteren Wolken,
durch Regenfluten rollt der Donner,
die Ulme,
wassergewaltig,
zittert in schwarzen Lachen des Himmels,
von Blitzen durchquert.

Die verbissene Ordnung des Landes.
Das Aufbegehren und die Macht.
Die Ohnmacht und die Kälte der Blitze.
Nicht reinigt der Regen die Atmosphäre.

Bei Wildenbruch

Eine Distel,
deren Gedächtnis der Wind zerfasert.

Pferde mit blitzenden
Brustblattgeschirren.

Im durchsonnten Wasser
der messerscharfe Schatten der Fische.

Bald frißt der Nebel
aus der Krippe kahler Äste.

Das Geständnis des Jahrs, die Krähen
tragen es in die weiße Finsternis des Himmels.

The muffled trombones
in the dark clouds,
thunder rolling through torrential rain,
the elm,
inundated,
shuddering in black puddles of sky,
criss-crossed by lightning.

The grim order of the country.
The power and the rebellion.
Impotence and the chill of lightning.
The air not cleansed by rain.

At Wildenbruch

A thistle,
its memory shredded in the wind.

Horses with flashing
breastplates on their harness.

In sun-lit water,
the razor-sharp shadows of fish.

Fog makes short work
of the manger of leafless boughs.

The year's confession—crows bear it away
into the pale gloom of sky.

April 63

Aufblickend vom Hauklotz
im leichten Regen,
das Beil in der Hand,
seh ich dort oben im breiten Geäst
fünf junge Eichelhäher.

Sie jagen lautlos, geben Zeichen
von Ast zu Ast,
sie weisen der Sonne
den Weg durchs Nebelgebüsch.
Und eine feurige Zunge fährt in die Bäume.

Ich bette mich ein
in die eisige Mulde meiner Jahre.
Ich spalte Holz,
das zähe splittrige Holz der Einsamkeit.
Und siedle mich an
im Netz der Spinnen,
die noch die Öde des Schuppens vermehren,
im Kiengeruch
gestapelter Zacken,
das Beil in der Hand.

Aufblickend vom Hauklotz
im warmen Regen des April,
seh ich an blanken
Kastanienästen
die leimigen Hüllen
der Knospen glänzen.

April 63

Looking up from the chopping-block
under a light rain,
with axe in hand,
I see up there in the wide boughs
five young jays.

In silence, they chase, they indicate
from branch to branch,
pointing a way for the sun
through the hazy undergrowth.
And a fiery tongue flashes among the trees.

I make my bed
in the icy hollow of my years.
I split logs,
the tough splintery wood of isolation.
And I settle myself
among spiders' webs,
deepening further the desolation of the shed,
among the odours of pine
piled rough-cuts
with axe in hand.

Looking up from the chopping-block
in warm April rain,
I see leafless
horse-chestnut boughs,
their sticky sheaths
of buds shine.

Waschtag

Die Eimer drämmern
aufs Pflaster, ich schütte
die Lauge aus,
das trübe Wasser
vertaner Zeit.
Ich spanne die Leine
von Baum zu Baum.

Ein schwarzer SIS mit weißen Gardinen
rollt suchend die Straße hinab
und hält vor meiner Tür.

Eine Granne,
nicht zugeweht
vom Sommer,
stachelt sich fest
in meiner Kehle.

Die Fähigkeit

Die Fähigkeit
der Dichterspinnen,
aus eigener Substanz
das dünne Seil zu drehen,
auf dem sie dann geschickt
mit zwei Gesichtern
und einer Feder
durch alle Lüfte balancieren.

Washday

The bucket's clank
on the pavement, I pour
out the suds,
the murky water
of wasted time.
I string a line
from tree to tree.

A black SIS with white drapes
rolls searching down the road
and stops at my door.

A chaff,
not blown there
by summer,
catches deep
in my throat.

The Knack

The knack
of poet-spiders—
to spin from their own
substance a thin wire
on which to balance
adroitly with two faces,
a single feather,
whatever the breeze.

Meinungen

Die Leute sagen im Ort:
Drei Kieselsteine,
vor eine Straßenwalze
geworfen.

Die Freunde sagen:
Tauwetter kommt
und legen beschneite Mäntel ab.

Einer, für Jahre
eingesessen in Bautzen,
stellt sich ans Fenster und liest.

Bald füllt sich das Zimmer
mit jungen und alten Stimmen,
mit Tabak und Asche,
mit Hoffnung und Zweifel.

Die Katzen,
die hinter der Tür
auf der Treppe dämmern,
sind weise und schweigen.

Pe-Lo-Thien

Laß mich bleiben
im weißen Gehölz,
Verwalter des Windes
und der Wolken. Erhell
die Gedanken einsamer Felsen.

Aus eisigen Wassern
tauchen die Tage auf,
störrisch und blind.
Mit geschundenen Masken

Opinions

Round here people say:
three pebbles
thrown down
in the path of a steamroller.

Friends tell me:
the thaw's coming
and they put aside their snow-caked jackets.

One, shut away
for years in Bautzen,
moves towards the window to read.

Soon the room fills
with voices of young and old,
with tobacco and ash,
with hope and doubt.

The cats, dozing
beyond the door
and up the stairs,
are wise and keep silent.

Pe-Lo-Thien

Let me remain here
in the white wood—
keeper of winds
and cloud—cast light
on thoughts of solitary cliffs.

Out of the freezing waters,
days emerge
stubborn and blind.
With their ravaged masks

suchen sie frierend
das dünne Reisigfeuer
des Verfemten,
der hinter der Mauer lebt
mit seinen Kranichen und Katzen.

Erscheinung der Nymphe im Ahornschauer

Von welchen Seen
und Schleiern aus Wasser
erhob sich dein Schatten,
von welchen Doggen gerissen,
stürztest du in die kiesige Grube?

Die Augen bedeckt
vom dünnen Messing
gezackter Blätter des Ahorns,
ist dir der Fischer entrückt,
der abends,
die Purpurschnecken im Korb,
zum Rauch seiner Hütte geht.
Es warten
die schwarzen Klippen,
die Süßwasserquellen
im Meer vor Kiveri.

they seek out
the meagre brushwood fire
of the outlaw
who lives beyond the wall
with his cranes and cats.

Vision of a Nymph in a Fall of Maple Leaves

From what lakes
and veils of water
did your shadow rise—
hounded by what mastiffs,
did you plunge into the gravel pit?

Your eyes blinded
with the fine brass
of serrated maple leaves,
the fisherman now eludes you,
at evening,
purple snails in his basket,
returning to the smoke of his cottage.
The black cliffs
are waiting,
the fresh water springs
in the sea off Kiveri.

Am Tage meines Fortgehns

Am Tage meines Fortgehns
entweichen die Dohlen
durchs glitzernde Netz der Mücken.

Am Acker klebt
der Rauch des Güterzuges,
der Himmel regenzwirnig,
dann grau gewalkt,
ein schweres Tuch,
niedergezogen
von der nassen Fahrspur.

Namen,
vernarbt und überwuchert
von neuen Zellen,
wie die verzerrte Schrift
im Baum—
ein eisiger Hauch
fegt über die Tenne der Worte.
Die Mittagsdistel erlosch
im heuigen Licht der Scheune.

Die leichte Dünung
wehender Gräser
verebbt an den Steinen.
Gealtert
geht das Jahr
mit stumpfer Axt, ein Tagelöhner,
auf den Spuren des Dachses
über die Hügel davon.
Die Leere saust
in den lehmigen Löchern
der Uferschwalben.

On the Day of My Leaving

On the day of my leaving,
jackdaws fleeing
through a glittering net of midges.

Smoke from a freight train
glued flat to the plough-land,
the sky rain-threaded,
then beaten grey,
a heavy cloth,
dragged low
across the sodden lane.

Names,
scarred and overgrown
with new cell growth,
like carved letters distorted
on a tree—
an icy breath
sweeps across the threshing-floor of words.
Midday's thistle withered
in the hay-light of the barn.

A faint swell
runs through wavering grasses,
ebbs against the stones.
Ancient,
the year proceeds
with its blunt axe, a journeyman,
on the badger's trail
over the hills and far away.
Emptiness roars
through the loamy burrows
of the sandmartins.

Hubertusweg

Märzmitternacht, sagte der Gärtner,
wir kamen vom Bahnhof
und sahen das Schlußlicht des späten Zuges
im Nebel erlöschen. Einer ging hinter uns,
wir sprachen vom Wetter.
Der Wind wirft Regen
aufs Eis der Teiche,
langsam dreht sich das Jahr ins Licht.

Und in der Nacht
das Sausen in den Schlüssellöchern.
Die Wut des Halms
zerreißt die Erde.
Und gegen Morgen wühlt
das Licht das Dunkel auf.
Die Kiefern harken Nebel von den Fenstern.

Dort unten steht,
armselig wie abgestandener Tabakrauch,
mein Nachbar, mein Schatten
auf der Spur meiner Füße, verlass ich das Haus.
Mißmutig gähnend
im stäubenden Regen der kahlen Bäume
bastelt er heute am rostigen Maschendraht.
Was fällt für ihn ab, schreibt er die Fahndung
ins blaue Oktavheft, die Autonummern meiner Freunde,
die leicht verwundbare Straße belauernd,
die Konterbande,
verbotene Bücher,
Brosamen für die Eingeweide,
versteckt im Mantelfutter.
Ein schwaches Feuer nähre mit einem Ast.

Ich bin nicht gekommen,
das Dunkel aufzuwühlen.
Nicht streuen will ich vor die Schwelle
die Asche meiner Verse,
den Eintritt böser Geister zu bannen.

Hubertusweg

March midnight, the gardener said,
as we came from the station,
seeing taillights of the late train
snuffed by fog. Someone walked behind us;
we spoke of the weather.
The wind throws rain
across the ice of the ponds,
the year spinning slowly towards the light.

And at night
the roaring at the keyholes.
The fury of stems
splitting the earth.
And come morning
light roots out the dark.
Pine trees rake mist from the windowpanes.

He stands down there,
wretched as stale tobacco smoke,
my neighbour, my shadow
on my heels as I leave the house.
Yawning sullenly
in flurries of rain from the bare trees,
he tinkers today with the rusty chicken wire.
What's in it for him, noting investigations
in his blue octavo book, my friends' car numbers,
keeping watch on this easily vulnerable street
for contraband,
forbidden books,
scraps for the belly,
stashed in a coat lining.
One branch to trouble a feeble fire.

I never came here
to stir up the darkness.
Nor will I scatter the ash of my verses
on the threshold
to bar entrance to evil spirits.

An diesem Morgen
mit nassem Nebel
auf sächsisch-preußischer Montur,
verlöschenden Lampen an der Grenze,
der Staat die Hacke,
das Volk die Distel,
steig ich wie immer
die altersschwache Treppe hinunter.

Vor der Keilschrift von Ras Schamra
seh ich im Zimmer meinen Sohn
den ugaritischen Text entziffern,
die Umklammerung
von Traum und Leben,
den friedlichen Feldzug des Königs Keret.
Am siebenten Tag,
wie IL der Gott verkündet,
kam heiße Luft und trank die Brunnen aus,
die Hunde heulten,
die Esel schrieen laut vor Durst.
Und ohne Sturmbock ergab sich eine Stadt.

Die Begrüssung

Am Zaun des Nachbarn vorbei,
argwöhnisch betrachtend
die Doppelreihe hoher Tulpen,
Meßlatte und Schnur verhalfen,
den richtigen Abstand zu nehmen,
gestutzte Taxushecken stehen wuchtig
im Rasen, grüne Marmorblöcke.

Noch halb im Schatten des Tulpenbeets,
sandig und heimlich angesiedelt
der Wegerich,
er hebt die rauhen Rispen
als Widerpart geharkter Ordnung.

This morning
with its damp fog
in Saxon-Prussian uniform,
lights are being extinguished at the border.
The state's a blade,
the people thistles.
I descend as usual
the decrepit stairs.

In his room I find my son
before the cuneiform script of Ras Shamra,
deciphering the Ugaritic text,
the communion
of life and dream,
the peaceful campaign of King Keret.
On the seventh day,
as the god IL proclaimed,
a hot wind blew and drank the wells dry,
the dogs howled,
the donkeys cried out with thirst.
And without the use of a battering ram the city surrendered.

The Greeting

There beyond my neighbour's fence,
gazing suspiciously
the double row of tall tulips,
distances precisely calculated
with the aid of rule and line,
the clipped yew hedges bulking large
by the lawn, green slabs of marble.

Still half in the shadow of the tulip beds,
establishing its secretive, sandy root
the plantain,
raising its rough panicles
as counterpart to the raked orderliness.

Die Begrüßung ist stumm
und brüderlich. Der Grubber liegt am Weg;
mit Eisenzähnen auszureißen
die Wurzeln erdiger Metaphern.

Unkraut

Auch jetzt, wo der Putz sich beult
und von der Mauer des Hauses blättert,
die Metastasen des Mörtels
in breiten Strängen sichtbar werden,
will ich mit bloßem Finger
nicht schreiben in die porige Wand
die Namen meiner Feinde.

Der rieselnde Schutt ernährt das Unkraut,
Brennesseln, kalkig blaß,
wuchern am rissigen Rand der Terrasse.
Die Kohlenträger, die mich abends
heimlich mit Koks versorgen,
die Körbe schleppen zur Kellerschütte,
sind unachtsam, sie treten
die Nachtkerzen nieder.
Ich richte sie wieder auf.

Willkommen sind Gäste,
die Unkraut lieben,
die nicht scheuen den Steinpfad,
vom Gras überwachsen.
Es kommen keine.

Es kommen Kohlenträger,
sie schütten aus schmutzigen Körben
die schwarze kantige Trauer
der Erde in meinen Keller.

The greeting is mute
and brotherly. A grubbing tool lies on the path.
With its iron teeth it will rip out
roots of earthy metaphors.

Weeds

Even now, when plaster flakes
and blows from the walls of this house,
the metastases of mortar
visible in thick ribbons,
with my bare finger I will not write
the names of my enemies
on the spongy wall.

Fallen rubble feeds the weeds,
nettles, chalky white,
teeming across the edge of the terrace.
The coalmen, who secretly
supply me with fuel in the evening,
hauling their baskets to the cellar chute,
are careless—they tread down
the evening primroses.
I coax them back up again.

Guests are always welcome,
those who love weeds,
those who do not shy away from stony paths
over-grown with grass.
No-one comes.

The coalmen come—
from their filthy baskets they pour
the lumpen black grief
of earth into my cellar.

Das Gericht

Nicht dafür geboren,
unter den Fittichen der Gewalt zu leben,
nahm ich die Unschuld des Schuldigen an.

Gerechtfertigt
durch das Recht der Stärke,
saß der Richter an seinem Tisch,
unwirsch blätternd in meinen Akten.

Nicht gewillt,
um Milde zu bitten,
stand ich vor den Schranken,
in der Maske des untergehenden Monds.

Wandanstarrend
sah ich den Reiter, ein dunkler Wind
verband ihm die Augen,
die Sporen der Disteln klirrten.
Er hetzte unter Erlen den Fluß hinauf.

Nicht jeder geht aufrecht
durch die Furt der Zeiten.
Vielen reißt das Wasser
die Steine unter den Füßen fort.

Wandanstarrend,
nicht fähig,
den blutigen Dunst
noch Morgenröte zu nennen,
hörte ich den Richter
das Urteil sprechen,
zerbrochene Sätze aus vergilbten Papieren.
Er schlug den Aktendeckel zu.

Unergründlich,
was sein Gesicht bewegte.
Ich blickte ihn an
und sah seine Ohnmacht.
Die Kälte schnitt in meine Zähne.

The Courtroom

Not made for this,
to live under the wings of violence,
I took on the innocence of a guilty man.

Justified
by the rule of might,
the judge sitting at his bench,
he leafed brusquely through my file.

Unwilling
to make a plea for clemency,
I stood before the bar,
in the mask of the waning moon.

Staring at the wall
I saw a horseman, a dark wind
blindfolding him,
the spurs of thistles clinking.
He sped off beneath the river alders.

Not everyone walks upright
through the ford of the times.
For many the current rips out stones
from beneath their feet.

Staring at the wall,
unable
to declare this bloody haze
the dawn,
I heard the judge
pronounce sentence,
broken phrases on yellowing papers.
He snapped the folder shut.

Inscrutable,
what moved across his face.
I looked up at him
and glimpsed his impotence.
Cold cut me to the teeth.

Notes on some of the poems

Arrival – See Isaiah 28, 1: "Woe to the crown of pride, to the drunkards of Ephraim, whose glorious beauty *is* a fading flower, which *are* on the head of the fat valleys of them that are overcome with wine!" (KJV)

Beside the Salmon Pool – Jean Améry was born Hans Mayer in 1912 in Vienna. Because of his Jewish background, he emigrated to Belgium in 1938 where he joined the Resistance. From 1943 to 1945 he was a prisoner in Auschwitz and Buchenwald. In 1978 he took his own life in Salzburg.

Pensione Cigolini – Huchel stayed at this pensione in Monterosso, near La Spezia, in 1959.

Midday in Succhivo – Gottfried Bermann Fischer (1897-1995) was a German publisher and owner of S. Fischer Verlag. He served in World War I and studied medicine at the universities of Breslau, Freiburg and Munich. After the Nazis came to power, Fischer moved from Berlin to Vienna and from there to Stockholm and the United States. He was the publisher of Huchel's second volume of poetry, *Chausseen Chaussen* (1963).

Subiaco – The Monastery of St Benedict is set high on a forested mountain cliff over Subiaco in central Italy. It enshrines the cave where St Benedict lived as a hermit before he organized his first monastic community. It is also the location of a famous fresco portrait of St Francis of Assisi.

These Numbered Days – See Isaiah 60, 20: "Thy sun shall no more go down; neither shall thy moon withdraw itself: for the LORD shall be thine everlasting light, and the days of thy mourning shall be ended." (KJV)

Estates – Several milk churns or cans, containing records of the struggle of the Jewish ghetto in Warsaw, were buried in the basement of a house on Nowolipki Street in 1942/3. The so-called Ringelbaum Archive was partially recovered in 1946 and 1950. Huchel visited Warsaw in 1956 and read about this archive in 1957.

On the Death of V.W. – Huchel seems here to be writing about the death of Virginia Woolf in 1941.

Where Eight Ways Meet – Søren Kierkegaard describes a path junction in Gribskov wood in Denmark where he liked to walk and to get lost. He called it the "Achtwegewinkel" or the angle/corner of eight ways. See Thyra Dohrenburg's translation into German at https://www.zeit.de/1950/23/acht-wege-und-die-einsamkeit.

M.V. – Huchel's wife said this poem was about his father (**M**ein **V**ater), who died in September 1945.

Before Nimes 1452 – This sequence alludes to the life of François Villon. He is portrayed as an exile, unwelcome in towns and moving through a hostile countryside. There are allusions to his gambling, a murder he committed and his escape from capital punishment.

Defeat – A Kremser was an old-fashioned, large horse-drawn carriage.

Middleham Castle – Before becoming king of England, Richard, Duke of Gloucester, spent several years of his childhood in the 1460s living in Middleham Castle, Wensleydale, Yorkshire.

Undine – Undines are elusive, female water nymphs associated with forest pools and waterfalls.

Beside Jordan – Abraham is said to have died at the age of 175 (Genesis, 25). Here, he recalls Hagar, the Egyptian handmaiden offered to him by his barren wife, Sarah, as a way of becoming a progenitor of nations, as God had promised him (Genesis, 16).

Alt-Seidenberg – The visionary figure here is Jakob Böhme who came from Alt-Seidenberg (modern Zawidow, Poland). In his childhood he tended cattle there. He also found a wooden container full of money but left it alone, an incident later interpreted as a sign of his future spiritual vocation.

Neighbours – Hermann Kesten (1900-1996) was a German novelist and dramatist, one of the principal figures of the New Objectivity movement in 1920s Germany. In 1933, when Hitler came to power, Kesten left Germany for Paris, then Amsterdam. In 1940, he emigrated to New York. He was active in PEN International and met Huchel in 1956 at a PEN conference. PEN International played an important role in securing Huchel's move to the West.

On the Road to Viznar – The soldiers in this poem are the Spanish Nationalists who shot Federico García Lorca on the road from Viznar to Alfacar in August 1936.

November – See Ezekiel 1, 1: "Now it came to pass in the thirtieth year, in the fourth *month*, in the fifth *day* of the month, as I *was* among the captives by the river of Chebar, *that* the heavens opened, and I saw visions of God". (KJV)

Snow – Hans Henny Jahnn (1894-1959) was a German playwright, novelist, organ-builder and music publisher. He went into exile in Bornholm. From 1950, he lived in Hamburg where he was President of the Free Academy of Arts. Huchel was also a member and became a close friend of Jahnn's. He published Jahnn's work several times in *Sinn und Form*.

The Angels – Though not made explicit in The Bible, the daughters of Cain were those "fair daughters of men" who by their lasciviousness caused the downfall of the "sons of God". See http://jewishencyclopedia.com/articles/3904-cain.

Aristeas – In the fourth book of his *Histories*, Herodotus tells of the death of the poet, Aristeas. He is said to have reappeared some 340 years later, claiming to have taken the form of a crow and to have been in the company of the god, Apollo. Huchel re-published this poem in his last book *Die neunte Stunde* (1979) with another poem on the same subject.

Farewell to Shepherds – Huchel was born under the astrological sign of Aries, the ram.

Copse – Heinrich Böll (1917-1985) was one of Germany's foremost post-World War II writers. He was awarded the Georg Buchner Prize in 1967 and the Nobel Prize for Literature in 1972. He visited Huchel several times during the period of his house arrest. Böll became president of PEN International. Together with Graham Greene, Arthur Miller and others, he managed to secure Huchel's release from the GDR.

Alkaios – Alkaios was a 7th century Greek poet whose work only survives in fragments. Huchel's interest in him relates to the image of him as an opponent of tyrannical rule, though he was defeated and sent into exile.

The Journey – Marie Luise Kaschnitz (1901-1974) was a German short story writer, novelist, essayist and poet. She was nominated for the 1967 Nobel Prize in Literature. She lived from the 1930s in Rome and Bollschweil, a village close to Staufen where Huchel lived from 1972-1981. They became close friends and Huchel edited a volume of her poetry for Suhrkamp Verlag.

The Order of the Storm – Saarmund is a village south of Wilhelmshorst; the Havel lakes are north of it. Huchel's house, in Wilhelmshorst, is almost exactly in the middle.

April 63 – April 1963 was not only the month that Huchel turned 60 but was also a period of harsh attacks from the GDR government. Several important writers and movie directors – Huchel being the most well-known – were denounced as traitors, as anti-communists, because of their freedom of artistic expression. As a result, no-one dared publish Huchel's work in the GDR.

Opinions – The three pebbles in this poem represent Huchel, his wife and their son. Bautzen was infamous in the GDR for its state security prisons. Bautzen I was used as an official prison, nicknamed *Gelbes Elend* ('Yellow Misery'), whereas the secret Bautzen II camp was for prisoners of conscience.

Pe-Lo-Thien – Pe-Lo-Thien was a poet and social critic of the Tang Dynasty. He spent six years living in exile. Huchel may well be drawing on Albert Ehrenstein's 1923 translations, published as *Pe-Lo-Thien: Nachdichtungen chinesischer Lyrik*.

Vision of a Nymph in a Fall of Maple Leaves – The submarine fresh water springs venting directly into the sea off Kiveri, Greece, have been known since antiquity.

Hubertusweg – This was Huchel's address when, in 1961, he was banished to effective house arrest in Wilhelmshorst. Every time he left the house, a Stasi spy followed him. Ugarit – often referred to as Ras Shamra, after the headland where it lies – was an ancient port in northern Syria on the outskirts of modern Latakia. Discovered in 1928, it also yielded up many Ugaritic cuneiform texts, revealing an otherwise unknown Northwest Semitic language. One of these texts was the *Epic of King Keret*.

Lightning Source UK Ltd.
Milton Keynes UK
UKHW040608170220
358841UK00001B/7